Book 6 - *in the "**End Times**" Series*

September 23-24, 2025: Millions Vanished in the Rapture – PART 2

How Hosea 6 Foretells 2,000 Years from Christ's Resurrection to His Return — and Why the Rapture Is September 23-24, 2025

By Mr. Elijah J Stone
and the Team Success Network

September 23-24, 2025: Millions Vanished in the Rapture

For permissions for this work to be reproduced, contact:
Team Success Network Publishing
Email: connect@teamsuccessnetwork.com

Published by Team Success Network Publishing
Printed in the United States of America

ISBN (Paperback): 978-1-968654-21-4
First Edition: September 2025

Cover Design by: Team Success Creative
Interior Layout by: Team Success Creative

Contact Us – Let's Build Together

This is more than a book. It's an invitation. A call to rise, to act, to build—together.

The "Team Success Network" exists to support churches, ministries, Christian groups, and all Christians -- as they pursue God's vision: bringing Heaven to Earth through unified, purpose-driven action. If this message stirs something in you, or if you're ready to explore what mutual success looks like in your community—we want to hear from you.

Let's start the conversation.

Reach out here:

📩 General Connection – connect@teamsuccessnetwork.com

📩 Share Your Team's Results & Testimonies – results@teamsuccessnetwork.com

📩 Submit Documents or Project Materials – docs@teamsuccessnetwork.com

📩 Contact Elijah Personally – elijah@teamsuccessnetwork.com

We're here to support, encourage, and collaborate. Whether you're just starting out or leading a growing movement—this is your first step. Let's build something eternal.

Table of Contents

PREFACE A – The Complete Prophecy Big Picture 8
PREFACE B – It Has To Happen, There Is No More Time.........................16

CHAPTER 1 – Hosea's Hidden Prophecy of Two Days..............................20
CHAPTER 2 – A Day as a Thousand Years: God's Prophetic Clock...........27
CHAPTER 3 – From Resurrection to Return: The 2,000-Year Span 35
CHAPTER 4 – Why AD 32 Matters: The Year of Christ's Resurrection 42
CHAPTER 5 – The Third Day: Messiah's Millennial Reign.........................50
CHAPTER 6 – Subtracting Seven Years: The Tribulation Factor 57
CHAPTER 7 – Why the Rapture Points to September 2025 64
CHAPTER 8 – What Will Happen When Millions Vanish 71
CHAPTER 9 – Living in the Final Hours Before the Trumpet 77
CHAPTER 10 – After the Rapture: A Message to the Left Behind 83
CHAPTER 11 – Life After the Rapture: The World in Chaos 89
CHAPTER 12 – The Bible's Prophecies Always Come True......................96

Preface A – The Complete Prophecy Big Picture

The Biblical Countdown to the Rapture and Christ's Reign

How Hosea's Prophecy and Daniel's Timeline Align with 2025

Setting the Stage

The Bible is a prophetic book from beginning to end. Its prophecies are not vague riddles; they are precise, unfolding on God's calendar with mathematical accuracy. Many of the prophecies that once seemed mysterious are becoming crystal clear now, because we are living in the last days.

This preface is designed to give you a step-by-step explanation of how one of the simplest but most profound prophecies — Hosea's "two days" — works together with the biblical principle of "a day = 1,000 years," and how it directly points us to the season we are in.

We will carefully walk through the verses, the logic, the history, and the prophetic timeline, so that you can see for yourself that the events of the Rapture and the coming Tribulation are not random guesses. They are laid out in Scripture.

Part 1 – The Prophetic Principle of Days

A Day = 1,000 Years

The first building block comes from the Scriptures themselves.

Psalm 90:4 says: *"For a thousand years in Your sight are like yesterday when it is past, and like a watch in the night."* Moses, the psalmist, reminds us that God does not measure time the way humans do. To Him, vast stretches of human history are like a single day.

Peter reaffirms this principle in the New Testament. In 2 Peter 3:8, he writes: *"But, beloved, do not forget this one thing, that with the Lord one day is as a thousand years, and a thousand years as one day."* This is not poetry alone. Peter says believers must **not forget** this truth.

Why? Because it explains God's timing in prophecy. People were already asking in Peter's day, "Where is the promise of His coming?" (2 Peter 3:4). Peter answers by showing that God measures days in thousand-year blocks.

The prophetic principle is simple but profound: **one day = 1,000 years** in God's prophetic calendar.

Hosea's Prophecy of Two Days

Now let's apply this principle to Hosea's prophecy.

Hosea 6:1–2 says: *"Come, and let us return to the Lord; for He has torn, but He will heal us; He has stricken, but He will bind us up. After two days He will revive us; on the third day He will raise us up, that we may live in His sight."*

This passage carries a dual meaning. On the surface, it was a call for Israel to repent in Hosea's own time. But prophetically, it looks forward to the long period of Israel's rejection of Messiah and the future restoration of the nation.

When we apply the prophetic principle — a day = 1,000 years — Hosea's "two days" become **2,000 years**. That means:

- After **two prophetic days (2,000 years)** from Christ's rejection, resurrection, and ascension, Israel will be revived.
- On the **third day (the third thousand years)**, Israel will "live in His sight" during the reign of Messiah — the Millennial Kingdom (Revelation 20:4–6).

This is a timeline prophecy. Hosea is not speaking of a short revival, but of a long span of history measured in God's days.

Prophetic Evidence from History

History fits this prophecy perfectly.

- Jesus was crucified and resurrected in **AD 32**.
- From that moment, the prophetic "two days" began.
- Add 2,000 years → you arrive at **AD 2032**.

This would be the hinge point for the prophecy's fulfillment: the revival of Israel and the visible return of Christ to reign.

This also agrees with the traditional understanding many prophecy teachers have long emphasized:

- **4,000 years** from Adam to Christ.
- **2,000 years** from Christ to His return.
- Total = **6,000 years** for humanity, followed by the 1,000-year Sabbath rest (the Millennial Kingdom).

So Hosea's prophecy aligns seamlessly with the broader biblical framework.

The Prophetic Tension

But there is a tension we need to resolve. Hosea points to **2032** as the year of Christ's visible return, 2,000 years after His resurrection. But we also know from Daniel and Revelation that before Christ returns to reign, there must first be a 7-year period of Tribulation.

This means we cannot simply stop at 2032. We must work backward. And when we do, the picture becomes even clearer.

Part 2 – The Countdown to September 23-24, 2025

Hosea's Two Days Point to 2032

Let's restate it clearly. Hosea 6:2 says: *"After two days He will revive us; on the third day He will raise us up, that we may live in His sight."*

- Two days = 2,000 years.

- Christ's resurrection = AD 32.
- Two days later = **AD 2032.**
- This is the appointed time for Israel's revival and Christ's visible reign.

But now we add the next piece: Daniel's prophecy of the Tribulation.

Subtracting the Tribulation

Daniel 9:27 says: *"Then he shall confirm a covenant with many for one week; but in the middle of the week he shall bring an end to sacrifice and offering."* This "week" refers to a seven-year period — the Tribulation.

Revelation 6–19 expands this picture, describing seals, trumpets, bowls, the rise of the Antichrist, and the suffering of the world during those seven years.

This period must occur before Christ's visible return. That means if Christ returns around **AD 2032**, we must subtract **7 years** for the Tribulation.

2032 – 7 = **2025.**

That means the Rapture — which occurs before the Tribulation — must happen in 2025.

The Feast of Trumpets Connection

Which day in 2025? The Feast of Trumpets provides the answer.

The Feast of Trumpets (Leviticus 23:23–25) is the appointed time for the blowing of trumpets to gather God's people. Paul ties this directly to the Rapture in 1 Thessalonians 4:16–17: *"For the Lord Himself will descend from heaven with a shout, with the voice of an archangel, and with the trumpet of God."*

In 2025, the Feast of Trumpets begins at sundown on September 22, following the new moon sighting. That means **September 23–24, 2025** is the second day of the Feast — the day most of the world will be observing it.

This is exactly what Brother Joshua testified: in 2018, Jesus appeared to him directly and told him the Rapture would occur on September 23–25, 2025. Seven years of warning — just as Noah was given seven days before the flood.

Daniel's 2,550-Day Proof

There is one more prophetic proof that locks this timeline in place: Daniel's count of days.

Daniel 12:11–12 says: *"And from the time that the daily sacrifice is taken away, and the abomination of desolation is set up, there shall be one thousand two hundred and ninety days. Blessed is he who waits, and comes to the one thousand three hundred and thirty-five days."*

Prophecy teachers like Medic4Christ on YouTube have shown that the Tribulation consists of **1,260 days (first half) + 1,290 days (second half) = 2,550 days.** This is exactly 7 years on the Jewish calendar.

Now here is the key: **only the year 2025 fits this prophecy exactly.** If the Tribulation begins at the Feast of Trumpets in September 2025, then 2,550 days later lands precisely on the **Day of Atonement in 2032.**

No other year aligns the Feast of Trumpets and the Day of Atonement with the 2,550-day count. Every other option fails. Only 2025–2032 works.

This means Hosea's broad prophecy, the 2,000-year principle, the subtraction of the Tribulation, and Daniel's 2,550 days all converge on the same timeline.

Prophetic Alignment

We can now summarize the alignment:

- **Hosea's "two days"** = 2,000 years from AD 32 → AD 2032.
- **Subtract 7 years for the Tribulation** = 2025.
- **Daniel's 2,550 days** = only 2025–2032 fits perfectly, ending on the Day of Atonement.
- **Feast of Trumpets 2025** = September 23–24, the day of the Rapture.
- **Brother Joshua's testimony** = direct revelation from Jesus confirming September 23-24, 2025.

All converge. All point to the same date. The Rapture will happen in 2025, followed by the Tribulation, and then Christ's visible return in 2032.

Why This Matters

The world is not prepared. Most churches are not prepared. Many mock or ignore prophecy. But God has spoken with clarity. Hosea, Daniel, Paul, John, and the testimony of faithful witnesses all agree.

This means the Rapture is not far off. It is near. It is at the door. Every moment matters now.

Closing Reflection

This is the prophetic puzzle completed:

- Hosea's "two days" point to 2032.
- Subtract the Tribulation, and you arrive at 2025.
- Daniel's 2,550 days prove 2025 is the only year that works.
- The Feast of Trumpets narrows it to September 23–24, 2025.
- Brother Joshua's testimony confirms it.

The Bible is not vague. God has not left us guessing. He has given us a clear, step-by-step calendar. Now the question is simple: **Will you be ready when the trumpet sounds?**

Preface B – It Has To Happen, There Is No More Time

The Final Date for the Rapture: September 23–24, 2025

The Last Warning Before the Trumpet Sounds

Why This Must Be Said

I'm going to speak plainly. There is no more time. The countdown has finished, the Scriptures line up, and the last trumpet is about to sound. The Rapture will happen on September 23–24, 2025. Not someday, not eventually, not maybe — it has to happen, and it will.

I am not giving you my opinion. I am laying out what the Bible says. The Word of God gives us the principle, the prophecy, and the proof. If you ignore this, you are ignoring the very voice of God.

The Day Equals a Thousand Years

Psalm 90:4 says, *"For a thousand years in Your sight are like yesterday when it is past."* Peter repeats it in 2 Peter 3:8, *"With the Lord one day is as a thousand years, and a thousand years as one day."* That is the foundation. That is the key.

One day in prophecy equals a thousand years. God told us exactly how to measure time. That means when Hosea says "two days," it means two thousand years. When Hosea says "the third day," it means the third thousand years. Simple. Exact. Undeniable.

Hosea's Prophecy

Hosea 6:2 says, *"After two days He will revive us; on the third day He will raise us up, that we may live in His sight."* There it is. After two prophetic days — 2,000 years — Israel will be revived. On the third day, Messiah will reign.

Jesus died and rose again in AD 32. Start the clock right there. Add two days — 2,000 years. That lands in AD 2032. That is the year of His visible return. The Word says it. History proves it. That's the anchor.

Subtract Seven Years

But here's the part most people miss. Before Jesus returns to reign, there must be seven years of Tribulation. Daniel 9:27 is clear: one final "week" of seven years. Revelation 6–19 spells it out in detail.

So you take the 2032 return and subtract seven years. That gives you 2025. Not 2026. Not 2024. Exactly 2025. And the Rapture must happen before that Tribulation begins.

The Feast of Trumpets

Now look at the calendar. In 2025, the Feast of Trumpets begins on September 22 at sundown in Israel. That means September 23 is the second day of the feast. That is the exact time when the trumpet sounds.

Paul says in 1 Thessalonians 4:16, *"For the Lord Himself will descend from heaven with a shout, with the voice of an archangel, and with the trumpet of God."* The trumpet is not random. The trumpet is tied to the Feast of Trumpets.

That's why the date is September 23–24, 2025. That is the day. That is the feast. That is the appointed time.

The Proof of 2,550 Days

Daniel 12:11–12 speaks of 1,290 days. Revelation 11 and 12 speak of 1,260 days. Add them together: 1,260 + 1,290 = 2,550 days. That is the exact length of the seven years.

Now listen closely: only the year 2025 to 2032 fits this count. Start at the Feast of Trumpets in September 2025, add 2,550 days, and you land exactly on the Day of Atonement in 2032. No other year works. Not 2024. Not 2026. Only 2025.

This is not my calculation. This is the Bible's calendar. And the math proves it.

No More Time

That is why I say this with urgency. It has to happen. There is no more time. All of prophecy — Hosea's two days, Daniel's 2,550 days, the Feast of Trumpets, and the testimony of Brother Joshua — converge on this one moment.

The Rapture will be September 23–24, 2025. That is the final date. That is the final warning. If you are not ready, you will be left behind.

What This Means For You

This is not a theory you can debate or a date you can push aside. This is the Word of God confirmed by history and prophecy. The reality is simple: September 23–24, 2025 is the dividing line between life as we know it and the chaos of the Tribulation.

If you are in Christ, this means your time to labor for the Kingdom is almost finished. You have days — not years — to share the Gospel, to repent of compromise, and to live with urgency. Every soul you reach now is one more soul snatched from the fire before the door shuts.

If you are not in Christ, this means the clock has run out. You cannot delay another moment. The trumpet will sound, and if you are not ready, you will be left behind to face seven years of terror under the rule of the Antichrist.

This is why the message is so direct: there is no more time. What you do right now will determine your eternity.

Closing Challenge

This is not a game. This is not speculation. This is not a maybe. This is prophecy, and it has to happen.

September 23–24, 2025 is the appointed time of the Rapture. The Bible proves it. The math confirms it. The Spirit has testified it. There is no more time.

The trumpet is about to sound. Are you ready?

Chapter 1 – Hosea's Hidden Prophecy of Two Days

Uncovering God's Timetable in a Single Verse

Why Hosea's Words Point to Our Generation

A Prophecy Hidden in Plain Sight

At first glance, Hosea 6:2 looks like a simple call to return to God. It reads: *"After two days He will revive us; on the third day He will raise us up, that we may live in His sight."* For centuries, people skimmed past this verse, taking it as a spiritual metaphor about renewal. But what if it is far more than that?

The Bible is filled with patterns where God hides prophetic truth inside everyday words. Jesus often spoke in parables, and prophets frequently used language that carried both immediate and future meaning. Hosea's words belong to this category. What looks like encouragement for Israel in his day is, in fact, a countdown for the world.

Hidden in those two phrases — "after two days" and "on the third day" — is the master clock of history. It points directly to the timeline between Christ's resurrection and His visible return. It shows that the

Rapture and Tribulation are not random events but part of God's precise schedule.

The Key of Prophetic Time

To unlock Hosea's words, we must first understand how God counts time. Scripture itself gives us the principle.

- **Psalm 90:4**: *"For a thousand years in Your sight are like yesterday when it is past, and like a watch in the night."*
- **2 Peter 3:8**: *"But, beloved, do not forget this one thing, that with the Lord one day is as a thousand years, and a thousand years as one day."*

This is the key. In prophecy, one day can equal a thousand years. This isn't guesswork; it is the way God Himself describes His perspective on time. Hosea's "two days" are not 48 hours — they are 2,000 years.

This principle also appears in the creation week. God made the world in six days and rested on the seventh. The pattern is prophetic: six "days" (6,000 years) for human history, then the seventh day (the 1,000-year reign of Christ). Hosea's prophecy fits this larger blueprint perfectly.

Hosea's Two Days

Hosea says, *"After two days He will revive us."* The context speaks of God's people being torn, wounded, and then healed. But in the prophetic timeline, it points to the two thousand years after Christ's death and resurrection.

From the moment Jesus rose in **AD 32**, the countdown began. Two thousand years forward brings us to **AD 2032**. That is the fulfillment of Hosea's "two days." At that time, Christ will return visibly to reign.

This means we are now living at the very end of the second day. The next major event is the transition into the "third day," the time when Messiah raises His people to live in His sight — the Millennial Kingdom.

The Third Day: Raised to Life

Hosea continues: *"On the third day He will raise us up, that we may live in His sight."* This is more than symbolic language. It describes the thousand-year reign of Christ on earth.

Revelation 20 confirms this: *"And they lived and reigned with Christ for a thousand years."* This is the third day — the day of resurrection, revival, and peace. After two thousand years of waiting, the world will finally see justice, healing, and restoration under the rule of Jesus.

For believers, this third day is the hope we long for. It is the time when tears will be wiped away, when creation itself will be restored, and when righteousness will cover the earth like water covers the sea. Hosea's "third day" is nothing less than the Millennium.

Why AD 32 Matters

Every prophecy needs a starting point. Hosea's countdown begins with Christ's resurrection. Historical evidence and prophetic alignment point to **AD 32** as the year when Jesus rose from the grave.

This year is not arbitrary. It fulfills Daniel's 70 weeks prophecy (Daniel 9:24–27) with exact precision. It also matches the historical Passover cycles and Roman records. In other words, AD 32 is the divinely appointed hinge of history.

From that year forward, God's prophetic clock has been counting. Add two thousand years, and the target is **AD 2032**. Subtract seven years for the Tribulation, and we arrive at **AD 2025** — the appointed time for the Rapture.

The Testimony of Brother Joshua

God confirms His Word not only through Scripture but also through testimony. On the YouTube channel *God's Voice Daily*, Brother Joshua from Africa shared how Jesus appeared to him face to face. This was not a dream or vision. Jesus Himself stood before him and told him the date of the Rapture: **September 23–25, 2025.**

This lines up perfectly with Hosea's prophecy. Two thousand years after AD 32 points to AD 2032 as the return. Subtract seven years for the Tribulation, and the Rapture falls exactly in 2025. What Joshua received by direct revelation matches what the Scriptures declare through prophecy.

This double witness — the Word and the testimony — removes all doubt. We are not guessing. We are declaring what God has appointed.

What the Rapture Will Look Like

The Rapture will be sudden, global, and undeniable. Paul describes it in 1 Thessalonians 4:16–17: *"For the Lord Himself will descend from heaven with a shout... and the dead in Christ will rise first. Then we who are alive and remain shall be caught up together with them in the clouds to meet the Lord in the air."*

In a single moment, millions of believers will vanish. All children under the age of accountability will be taken. Families will be torn apart. Pilots will disappear mid-flight, drivers will vanish mid-road, and the world will plunge into chaos.

This is not science fiction. It is prophecy. The world will never recover from the shock of that day.

The Global Chaos to Follow

Imagine the chain reaction:

- Planes plummeting without pilots.
- Cars crashing without drivers.
- Hospitals losing doctors and nurses.
- Governments missing key leaders.
- Homes shattered as children and spouses vanish.

The economy will collapse overnight. Technology will fail as a worldwide EMP strikes, leaving electronics burned out forever. Darkness will cover the earth for three days as demonic forces are unleashed. This will not just be a spiritual event — it will reshape every part of human life.

By 2026, the world will be unrecognizable. Life will never return to "normal."

The Tribulation Begins

After the Rapture, the world will enter the seven-year Tribulation. This is described in Revelation 6–19 and by Jesus in Matthew 24. It will be a time of deception, famine, war, plagues, and persecution.

The Antichrist will rise with promises of peace but will enslave humanity with fear. He will demand worship, control the economy, and enforce the mark of the beast. Those who refuse will be hunted, but those who resist will be saved eternally.

This time is unavoidable. It has been appointed in prophecy. Hosea's two days guarantee it.

Why This Matters to You

If you are reading this before the Rapture, you are living in the most critical moment in history. The countdown is nearly over. We have less than two weeks before September 23–25, 2025.

Now is the time to decide. Will you be taken, or will you be left behind? Will you surrender to Christ, or will you risk the horrors of the Tribulation?

The choice is urgent. The trumpet is about to sound.

Key Takeaways from Hosea's Prophecy

1. **Hosea 6:2 is not symbolic only.** It is a prophetic calendar.
2. **Two days = 2,000 years.** From Christ's resurrection in AD 32 to His return in AD 2032.
3. **The third day = 1,000 years.** The Millennial reign of Christ.

4. **Subtract seven years.** The Tribulation means the Rapture must happen in 2025.
5. **Confirmed by testimony.** Brother Joshua's vision matches the timeline exactly.

What to Do Now

- **Repent.** Turn from sin and surrender to Jesus.
- **Prepare.** Live ready for the trumpet call.
- **Warn others.** Share this truth before it is too late.
- **Trust God.** He has already revealed the plan.

The countdown is almost finished. Hosea's prophecy has brought us to the edge of eternity. The question is: **Are you ready?**

Chapter 2 – A Day as a Thousand Years: God's Prophetic Clock

How God Measures Time Differently Than We Do

Unlocking the Key That Explains Hosea's Prophecy

Why We Must See Time Through God's Eyes

If we want to understand prophecy, we cannot look at time the way humans normally do. We think in hours, days, weeks, and years. God, however, sees all of history from beginning to end in a single sweep. For Him, the passing of centuries is like the blink of an eye.

This is why the Bible gives us clues about how God measures time. Without these keys, Hosea's prophecy of "two days" would seem vague and mysterious. With them, however, everything becomes clear. What looks like poetry suddenly becomes a countdown with exact precision.

God does not leave His people in the dark. He reveals His timetable through patterns, symbols, and prophetic parallels. The principle of "a day as a thousand years" is one of the most important of these. It appears multiple times in Scripture, confirming that this is how we should read Hosea's prophecy.

The Witness of Scripture

The principle appears first in the Old Testament.

- **Psalm 90:4** – *"For a thousand years in Your sight are like yesterday when it is past, and like a watch in the night."*
- **Ecclesiastes 3:11** reminds us, *"He has made everything beautiful in its time; also He has put eternity in their hearts."* God's timekeeping is eternal, not bound by our clocks.

In the New Testament, Peter echoes the same truth:

- **2 Peter 3:8** – *"But, beloved, do not forget this one thing, that with the Lord one day is as a thousand years, and a thousand years as one day."*

Peter was speaking to believers who were discouraged that Christ had not yet returned. He reminded them that God's promises operate on His prophetic timetable. What feels like delay to us is simply God's precise plan unfolding.

When Hosea wrote of "two days," he was not speaking casually. He was declaring two prophetic days, equal to two thousand years. God Himself defined the scale.

The Creation Week Pattern

God also revealed this principle in creation itself. He created the world in six days and rested on the seventh. Each of those days becomes a prophetic model of one thousand years.

- **Day 1–6** = Six thousand years of human history.

- **Day 7** = The seventh "day," or the Millennial reign of Christ — one thousand years of rest.

This pattern is woven throughout Scripture. Hebrews 4 speaks of a "rest" still waiting for the people of God. Revelation 20 describes the thousand-year reign. Hosea points directly to this "third day," the day of revival and living in God's sight.

The creation week is more than history; it is prophecy in miniature. God was showing us from the beginning how He would govern time.

The Rhythm of Prophetic Days

Think about how this plays out:

- From Adam to Abraham = roughly two thousand years (two days).
- From Abraham to Christ = roughly two thousand years (two days).
- From Christ's resurrection to His return = two thousand years (two days).
- Then comes the final "day" — the Millennial reign (one day).

This adds up to seven thousand years, a complete cycle that matches God's perfect number. Hosea's "two days" fit into this structure perfectly. They describe the period between Christ's resurrection and His visible return.

When we read Hosea's words with this principle, everything lines up. Without it, we miss the entire meaning.

Why Human Timekeeping Fails

Humans think of time in terms of schedules and calendars. We measure minutes, hours, and days. But human calendars shift. Some cultures used lunar calendars, others solar, and leap years were added to correct the drift. Even today, nations use different systems to mark years.

God, however, does not measure time with our imperfect tools. His timeline is eternal, exact, and unchanging. His prophetic days are never shortened or lengthened by leap years or human adjustments.

When He says "two days," He means exactly two thousand years. His calendar is perfect, and His plan never drifts off course.

Why This Matters for Prophecy

Without this principle, Hosea 6:2 would simply sound like spiritual encouragement. But with it, we realize it is a countdown.

- **Two days = 2,000 years from Christ's resurrection.**
- **Third day = 1,000-year Millennial reign.**

This means we can pinpoint the season of Christ's return. It's not guesswork. It's not speculation. It's a timetable written into the very structure of Scripture.

God wants His people to know the times and seasons. Jesus rebuked the Pharisees for knowing how to read the weather but not how to read the signs of the times (Matthew 16:3). Understanding prophetic time allows us to see exactly where we stand in history.

Hosea's Prophecy in Context

Hosea lived during a time of national rebellion. His prophecies often focused on Israel's sin and God's coming judgment. Yet in the middle of his warnings, he gave glimpses of hope — promises of restoration. Hosea 6:1–2 is one of those.

For his audience, it meant that after a period of judgment, God would heal and restore His people. But for us, it carries a much larger meaning. When read through the lens of "a day = 1,000 years," it becomes a prophecy for all humanity.

It tells us that God set the timeline long ago. He promised restoration "after two days" — after two thousand years from the resurrection. And He promised the glory of His presence "on the third day."

Why AD 32 Anchors the Clock

The resurrection of Jesus in AD 32 is the starting point for Hosea's prophecy. That was the moment God's plan reached its turning point. Death was defeated, sin was conquered, and eternal life was made possible.

From that moment, the "two days" began counting forward. Every year since AD 32 has been part of that countdown. And now we are nearing the end.

This means prophecy is not vague. It is precise. It shows us that God has an appointed time for the Rapture, the Tribulation, and the return of Christ.

How This Strengthens Faith

Understanding God's prophetic clock gives believers confidence. The world looks chaotic, but history is not random. God is moving it forward exactly as He planned.

Every war, every empire, every revival, and every fall fits into the two days of waiting. Nothing has been wasted. Everything is on schedule.

For us, this means we do not have to fear the future. God already told us the end from the beginning. Hosea's prophecy is proof that He is in control of time itself.

A Warning to the World

For unbelievers, this truth is a warning. The two days are nearly complete. The countdown is almost finished. Soon the trumpet will sound, and the Rapture will take place.

Many will be caught off guard. They will think life will continue as always. But the day of the Lord will come suddenly, like a thief in the night (1 Thessalonians 5:2).

Understanding God's prophetic clock removes excuses. People cannot say they were not warned. The Scripture has been clear all along.

How to Live in Light of Prophetic Time

Knowing that we are at the end of the second day should change the way we live.

- **Urgency:** We don't have time to waste on sin or compromise.
- **Readiness:** We must live as if the trumpet could sound at any moment.

- **Mission:** We must share the gospel while there is still time.
- **Hope:** We know the suffering of this world is temporary, and the third day is coming.

This is not just theology. It is a lifestyle. Understanding prophetic time demands that we live differently.

Key Points to Remember

1. Hosea's "two days" are two thousand years.
2. This principle is confirmed in Psalm 90:4 and 2 Peter 3:8.
3. The creation week models the same pattern of six days plus a seventh.
4. Christ's resurrection in AD 32 is the anchor point.
5. Two thousand years from then = AD 2032, the time of His return.
6. Subtract seven years for the Tribulation = AD 2025, the time of the Rapture.

A Call to Action

The prophetic clock is almost at midnight. The two days are nearly complete. The trumpet is about to sound.

If you are reading this before the Rapture, you must take this seriously. Repent of sin, surrender to Jesus, and live ready. If you are reading this after the Rapture, know that this book was written to explain exactly why millions vanished.

God has always kept His Word. Hosea's prophecy is being fulfilled before our eyes. The question is: will you be found ready when time runs out?

Chapter 3 – From Resurrection to Return: The 2,000-Year Span

How Hosea's Two Days Outline the Age of the Church

Why 2032 Marks the End of the Waiting Period

The Resurrection as the Starting Point

Every prophetic timeline needs a starting point. For Hosea's prophecy, the starting point is not random — it is the most important event in human history: the resurrection of Jesus Christ.

On that third day in AD 32, the Son of God rose from the grave. Death was conquered, sin was defeated, and eternal life was secured for all who believe. But it was also the moment that set the prophetic countdown of Hosea 6:2 into motion: *"After two days He will revive us; on the third day He will raise us up, that we may live in His sight."*

From the resurrection forward, history entered into the age of waiting — two prophetic days, equal to 2,000 years. This is the span of time we are living in now, often called the "Church Age." It stretches from AD 32 until AD 2032, when the two days are complete.

Why Hosea's Prophecy Begins Here

Some might ask, "Why start with the resurrection and not the birth of Christ?" The answer is found in Scripture itself.

- Paul wrote in Romans 1:4 that Jesus was *"declared to be the Son of God with power according to the Spirit of holiness, by the resurrection from the dead."*
- The resurrection was the proof of His identity and the beginning of the new covenant.
- The resurrection fulfilled prophecy and began the countdown to His return.

The birth of Christ was miraculous, but the resurrection was the hinge of history. It was the victory moment, the day Satan was defeated and God's prophetic timetable was sealed.

The Two Thousand-Year Countdown

From AD 32, Hosea's "two days" equal exactly 2,000 years. That means the prophetic countdown stretches all the way to AD 2032.

- **Day One (AD 32–1032):** The gospel spreads from Jerusalem to the ends of the earth. Persecutions come, the Roman Empire falls, and the Church takes root.
- **Day Two (AD 1032–2032):** The Church continues through reformations, awakenings, revivals, and missionary movements. The world is transformed by the spread of the gospel, yet also marked by wars and sin.

Now we are at the end of the second day. The 2,000-year span is almost complete. The return of Christ is no longer distant; it is at the doorstep.

Why AD 2032 Is the Target

If Jesus rose in AD 32, then two thousand years forward brings us to AD 2032. That is the completion of Hosea's "two days."

This aligns with the Hosea prophecy perfectly:

- *"After two days He will revive us"* — revival, restoration, and resurrection come after the two thousand years.
- *"On the third day He will raise us up"* — the Millennium, the thousand-year reign of Christ, begins.

This means AD 2032 is not just another year. It is the prophetic end of the waiting period, the moment when history transitions into the reign of Messiah.

The Church Age in Prophecy

The 2,000-year span from resurrection to return is also described in other parts of the Bible.

- Jesus spoke of the **"times of the Gentiles"** (Luke 21:24) — a period when the gospel would go to the nations before Israel's full restoration.
- Paul described the **"mystery of Christ"** revealed in the Church (Ephesians 3:4–6).

- Revelation 2–3 shows the seven letters to the churches, often seen as a prophetic outline of the entire Church Age.

Hosea's "two days" are another way of describing the same period. From resurrection to return, the Church Age spans exactly 2,000 years.

What This Means for Us Today

We are not at the beginning of the story. We are at the end of the two days. Nearly 2,000 years have passed since Christ rose, and only a short time remains before His visible return.

This means we are the generation that will see the fulfillment of Hosea's prophecy. We are living in the final hours of the second day. That is why the urgency is so great.

The Tribulation Factor

The return of Christ at AD 2032 is the visible return, when He reigns on earth. But before that comes the seven-year Tribulation. Daniel 9:27 describes a covenant broken halfway through seven years. Revelation 6–19 describes seals, trumpets, and bowls of judgment poured out on the earth.

This means the Rapture must take place seven years earlier, in AD 2025. The Church will be taken before the wrath of God falls. The countdown from resurrection to return proves this with exact precision.

- Resurrection = AD 32.
- Return = AD 2032.
- Subtract 7 years = Rapture in AD 2025.

The two-day prophecy points directly to our moment in history.

A Warning to the Skeptics

Some will say, "No one knows the day or the hour" (Matthew 24:36). That is true. But Jesus also commanded us to know the times and seasons (Matthew 16:3; 1 Thessalonians 5:1–4). Hosea's prophecy does not give us the exact hour, but it does reveal the appointed season.

The fact that all timelines converge on 2025–2032 cannot be coincidence. Hosea, Daniel, Revelation, and even the testimony of modern witnesses like Brother Joshua all confirm it. To dismiss this is to ignore the Word of God.

How We Should Live in the Countdown

Knowing we are at the end of the two days should change everything about the way we live.

- **Repentance:** We must turn away from sin and live holy lives.
- **Urgency:** We cannot delay; the trumpet is near.
- **Mission:** We must share the gospel with as many as possible before the Rapture.
- **Hope:** We know that our suffering is temporary and that the third day is coming soon.

The countdown is almost over. We cannot live as if life will continue forever as it has.

Key Scriptures for the Two Days

- **Hosea 6:2** – The central prophecy.
- **Psalm 90:4** – A day is as a thousand years.
- **2 Peter 3:8** – Confirming the principle of prophetic time.
- **Revelation 20:4** – The thousand-year reign (third day).
- **Romans 1:4** – The resurrection as the declaration of Christ's Sonship.

Together, these verses build the case. From resurrection to return is two prophetic days, 2,000 years exactly.

What Will Happen After 2032

Hosea says, *"On the third day He will raise us up."* The third day is the Millennium, when Christ reigns for 1,000 years.

This is the time when Israel will be restored, the nations judged, and creation itself renewed. It is the fulfillment of promises made to Abraham, David, and the prophets. It is the day when righteousness covers the earth.

This third day is what we long for. The two days of waiting lead to the greatest day of all — the day when we live in His sight.

Summary of the 2,000-Year Span

1. **Start:** Resurrection of Christ in AD 32.
2. **Span:** Two prophetic days = 2,000 years.

3. **End:** Visible return of Christ in AD 2032.
4. **Tribulation:** Seven years before return = Rapture in 2025.
5. **Third Day:** Millennium begins after the two days.

This is the prophetic span Hosea described in one verse.

Final Call

We are at the end of the second day. The Rapture is nearly upon us. The return of Christ is only a few years away.

If you are reading this before the Rapture, the time to act is now. Repent, believe, and prepare your heart for the trumpet. If you are reading this after the Rapture, know that Hosea's words have been fulfilled. You must endure the Tribulation and refuse the mark of the beast.

The 2,000-year span is proof that God has always been in control. History is not random. It is prophetic. And you are living at the very edge of time.

Chapter 4 – Why AD 32 Matters: The Year of Christ's Resurrection

The Anchor Point for God's Prophetic Timeline

How One Date Unlocks the Mystery of Hosea's Prophecy

Why This Date Is the Hinge of History

When it comes to prophecy, details matter. God is not vague or careless about His appointed times. He set the exact year of Christ's death and resurrection, and He built the prophetic calendar around it. That year is **AD 32**.

This was the year when the Son of God rose from the grave. The resurrection was not just a miracle; it was the anchor point for the rest of human history. Every prophecy about the end times begins here. Hosea's "two days" cannot be measured without this starting point.

AD 32 is more than a date on a calendar. It is the dividing line between life and death, between the old covenant and the new, between prophecy fulfilled and prophecy yet to come. Without understanding this date, we cannot fully grasp God's prophetic plan.

The Prophetic Significance of the Resurrection

The resurrection was the central event of Scripture. Paul wrote in 1 Corinthians 15:17: *"If Christ is not risen, your faith is futile; you are still in your sins!"* Everything hinges on that morning.

- The resurrection proved that Jesus is the Son of God (Romans 1:4).
- It fulfilled Old Testament prophecies (Psalm 16:10; Isaiah 53).
- It marked the victory over death and sin.
- It began the prophetic "two days" of Hosea's timeline.

The cross was the payment, but the resurrection was the receipt. It confirmed everything Jesus said and did. It is the day when prophecy moved from promise to fulfillment.

Why AD 32 and Not Another Year?

Some scholars argue for AD 30 or AD 33 as the year of Christ's death and resurrection. But when all evidence is examined — both biblical and historical — AD 32 emerges as the most accurate.

1. **Daniel's 70 Weeks Prophecy (Daniel 9:24–27):**
    - The prophecy counts forward from the decree to rebuild Jerusalem in 445 BC.
    - 483 years later (69 "weeks") brings us exactly to AD 32.

   - This aligns perfectly with the year of Christ's crucifixion and resurrection.

2. **Passover Timing:**
   - The crucifixion had to occur during Passover, the 14th day of Nisan.
   - Astronomical calculations place Passover on April 10, AD 32, which matches the gospel accounts.

3. **Roman Historical Records:**
   - Pontius Pilate governed Judea from AD 26–36.
   - The crucifixion falls exactly in the middle of his tenure.

All evidence converges on AD 32. It is the year that fits Daniel's prophecy, the Jewish feast cycle, and the Roman records.

AD 32 as the Starting Point of Hosea's Two Days

Now that we know AD 32 is the resurrection year, we can see how Hosea's prophecy applies.

- Hosea 6:2: *"After two days He will revive us; on the third day He will raise us up, that we may live in His sight."*
- A day = 1,000 years (Psalm 90:4; 2 Peter 3:8).
- Two days = 2,000 years.
- 2032 = the visible return of Christ.
- Subtract 7 years for Tribulation = 2025, the Rapture.

AD 32 is not just the year of resurrection. It is the year God's prophetic clock started counting toward the end of the age.

The Resurrection and Israel's Timeline

AD 32 was not only about the Church — it was also about Israel.

- Jesus predicted that Jerusalem would be destroyed (Luke 21:20–24). This happened in AD 70.
- Hosea's prophecy speaks of revival after two days. That includes Israel's revival in the last days.
- The scattering of Israel began after the resurrection, and their restoration will come at the end of the two thousand years.

This means AD 32 is also the point where Israel's prophetic story took a new direction. It marked the time of their scattering, but it also pointed toward their future restoration.

The Feast Days as Prophetic Markers

The feasts of Israel are prophetic shadows of Christ's work. AD 32 shows how perfectly they align.

- **Passover (Nisan 14):** Jesus crucified as the Lamb of God.
- **Unleavened Bread (Nisan 15):** His sinless body in the tomb.
- **Firstfruits (Nisan 16):** His resurrection as the firstfruits of the dead (1 Corinthians 15:20).

- **Pentecost (50 days later):** The Holy Spirit poured out on the Church.

AD 32 fulfilled the spring feasts to the exact day. This proves God's timing is exact, not approximate. It also means the fall feasts — Trumpets, Atonement, Tabernacles — will be fulfilled just as precisely in the last days.

The Prophetic Timeline from AD 32

When we use AD 32 as the anchor, the rest of the prophetic timeline becomes clear.

- **AD 32:** Resurrection of Christ.
- **AD 70:** Destruction of Jerusalem and scattering of Israel.
- **AD 1804–2025:** The 28th "time" from Ecclesiastes, the final prophetic season.
- **September 23–25, 2025:** The Rapture of the Church (Feast of Trumpets).
- **AD 2025–2032:** Seven-year Tribulation.
- **AD 2032:** Visible return of Christ and the start of the Millennium.

Every major prophetic event flows from the resurrection in AD 32.

Why This Matters to Believers

AD 32 is not just a date for scholars. It matters for every believer because it proves God's plan is exact.

- Your faith is not based on guesswork.
- Prophecy is not vague but precise.
- The countdown to Christ's return is real and measurable.

When you understand why AD 32 matters, you realize that we are at the very end of the two days. The Rapture is not far off. The trumpet could sound at any moment.

What Happens If You Ignore the Date?

Many Christians do not care about prophecy. They say, "It doesn't matter when it happens — I'll be ready whenever." But Jesus warned us to watch and be ready.

- Matthew 24:42 – *"Watch therefore, for you do not know what hour your Lord is coming."*
- Revelation 3:3 – *"If you will not watch, I will come upon you as a thief, and you will not know what hour I will come upon you."*

Ignoring prophecy leads to complacency. Understanding AD 32 leads to urgency.

The Testimony of History

Look at what has happened since AD 32:

- The gospel has spread to every continent.

- Israel has been scattered and restored.
- The Church has gone through persecution, reformations, and revivals.
- Technology now allows global communication and control, fulfilling Revelation's prophecies.

All of this happened within the two days of Hosea's prophecy. None of it is coincidence. It all flows from the resurrection in AD 32.

A Call to Repentance and Readiness

We are nearing the end of the timeline. The trumpet is about to sound. The Rapture is less than two weeks away.

If you are reading this before September 23–25, 2025, you must repent and prepare now. Do not assume you have time. The clock that started in AD 32 is about to strike midnight.

If you are reading this after the Rapture, know that what happened was not random. It was the fulfillment of prophecy. You must endure the Tribulation, reject the mark of the beast, and cling to Christ no matter the cost.

Key Takeaways

1. **AD 32 is the year of Christ's resurrection.**
2. **It fulfills Daniel's 70 Weeks prophecy.**
3. **It aligns with the Jewish feast calendar.**

4. **It is confirmed by Roman history.**
5. **It is the anchor for Hosea's "two days."**
6. **It points to AD 2032 as Christ's return and AD 2025 as the Rapture.**

Closing Reflection

AD 32 was the year the world changed forever. It was the day death lost its power and eternal life became possible. But it was also the day the prophetic clock began to count toward the end of the age.

We are now standing at the end of that countdown. The Rapture is near. The return of Christ is at hand. Hosea's words are being fulfilled in our generation.

The question is simple: **Are you ready for what comes next?**

Chapter 5 – The Third Day: Messiah's Millennial Reign

Hosea's Prophecy of Revival Fulfilled

The Thousand-Year Day of Christ's Rule

The Third Day in Hosea's Prophecy

Hosea's prophecy does not stop at two days. After telling us that God would revive His people "after two days," he continues: *"On the third day He will raise us up, that we may live in His sight"* (Hosea 6:2).

This is one of the clearest pictures of the Millennium in the Old Testament. After two prophetic days (2,000 years from Christ's resurrection), comes the third prophetic day — a thousand years when God raises His people up and they live in His presence.

This third day is the reign of Messiah on earth. It is the fulfillment of countless promises: to Israel, to the Church, and to creation itself. It is the time of peace, justice, and restoration that every believer has longed for.

The Pattern of the Days

We have already seen the pattern of prophetic days:

- **Day 1–2 (Adam to Abraham):** Foundations laid.
- **Day 3–4 (Abraham to Christ):** Israel chosen, covenant made.
- **Day 5–6 (Christ to present):** Church age, gospel spread.
- **Day 7 (The Millennium):** Christ reigns, rest for the world.

Hosea's "third day" fits into this pattern. After the two days of waiting since the resurrection (AD 32–2032), comes the thousand-year reign of Christ. The whole of Scripture points toward this day.

The Millennium in Revelation

The book of Revelation describes this reign explicitly.

- **Revelation 20:4** – *"And they lived and reigned with Christ for a thousand years."*
- **Revelation 20:6** – *"Blessed and holy is he who has part in the first resurrection. Over such the second death has no power, but they shall be priests of God and of Christ, and shall reign with Him a thousand years."*

This thousand-year reign is the third day Hosea foretold. It is the day when God's people are raised up to live in His sight. It is the fulfillment of promises made throughout the Bible.

Promises to Israel

The Millennium fulfills the promises made to Israel.

- God promised Abraham that his descendants would inherit the land forever (Genesis 17:8).
- God promised David that his throne would be established forever (2 Samuel 7:16).
- The prophets foretold a time when Israel would be restored, the nations would come to Jerusalem, and Messiah would reign.

During the Millennium, these promises will come true. Israel will be the head, not the tail. The Messiah will reign from Jerusalem, and the nations will stream to Him.

Promises to the Church

The Millennium also fulfills promises to the Church.

- Jesus promised that His followers would sit on thrones and judge the twelve tribes of Israel (Matthew 19:28).
- Paul wrote that the saints will judge the world and even angels (1 Corinthians 6:2–3).
- Revelation says believers will reign with Christ as kings and priests (Revelation 5:10).

The Church, taken in the Rapture, will return with Christ at His visible coming. We will reign with Him on earth for a thousand years. Hosea's words about being "raised up to live in His sight" describe this reality perfectly.

Promises to Creation

The Millennium will not only transform Israel and the Church — it will also renew creation itself.

- Isaiah 11:6–9 describes a world where the wolf lies with the lamb, and the earth is full of the knowledge of the Lord.
- Romans 8:21 says creation itself will be delivered from corruption into the glorious liberty of the children of God.
- Zechariah 14 describes living waters flowing from Jerusalem, transforming the land.

The third day is not only a spiritual revival but a physical one. The curse will be lifted, and the world will flourish as it was meant to from the beginning.

Why the Millennium Matters

Some dismiss the Millennium as symbolic. But Scripture makes it clear that it is literal. Six times in Revelation 20, the text says "a thousand years." Hosea's third day confirms it.

The Millennium matters because it shows that God keeps His promises. He made covenants with Abraham, David, Israel, and the Church. The Millennium is when all those covenants come true.

It also matters because it gives us hope. The suffering and injustice of this age will not last forever. Christ will reign, and everything will be set right.

The Transition into the Third Day

The third day begins after the Tribulation. At the end of the seven years, Christ returns visibly with His saints. He defeats the Antichrist and his armies at Armageddon (Revelation 19:19–21). Satan is bound and cast into the abyss for a thousand years (Revelation 20:1–3).

Then begins the reign of peace. The nations will be ruled with a rod of iron (Psalm 2:9; Revelation 19:15). Justice will cover the earth, and the knowledge of the Lord will fill every nation.

This is the day Hosea foresaw — the day when God raises His people up to live in His sight.

The Blessings of the Third Day

The Millennium will bring blessings beyond imagination:

- **Peace:** No more wars or violence. Nations will beat their swords into plowshares (Isaiah 2:4).
- **Justice:** Christ will rule with righteousness. No corruption, no oppression.
- **Healing:** The desert will blossom, and sickness will vanish (Isaiah 35:1, 5–6).
- **Joy:** People will live long lives in safety and prosperity (Isaiah 65:20–23).
- **Presence:** Most of all, God's presence will dwell visibly on the earth.

This is the day we are waiting for. The third day is the answer to centuries of longing.

Living in Light of the Third Day

For believers today, the promise of the third day should shape how we live.

- **Hope:** No matter how dark the world becomes, the Millennium is coming.
- **Patience:** The two days of waiting are almost over. Endure to the end.
- **Faith:** God has kept every promise so far; He will keep this one too.
- **Urgency:** Share the gospel while there is still time. The Rapture is almost here.

We live at the edge of history. The third day is only years away.

The Prophetic Timeline Summarized

- **AD 32:** Christ's resurrection. Hosea's "two days" begin.
- **AD 32–2032:** Two days (2,000 years) of waiting, the Church Age.
- **September 23–25, 2025:** The Rapture, beginning the Tribulation.
- **AD 2025–2032:** Seven years of judgment on earth.
- **AD 2032:** Christ returns visibly, defeating His enemies.
- **AD 2032–3032:** The Millennium — the third day of Hosea's prophecy.

This is the framework of God's plan. It is exact, unshakable, and nearly complete.

What About You?

The third day is coming whether you are ready or not. The only question is where you will stand.

- Will you be caught up in the Rapture to return with Christ in glory?
- Or will you be left behind to suffer through the Tribulation, only to face judgment?

Now is the time to decide. Now is the time to repent and surrender to Christ. Hosea's prophecy leaves no room for delay.

Closing Reflection

Hosea saw it long ago: two days of waiting, then a third day of glory. We are living at the very end of the second day. The trumpet is about to sound, and the third day is about to dawn.

The Millennium is not a myth. It is not a dream. It is the next chapter of history. Christ will reign, and His people will live in His sight.

The question is simple: **Will you be part of that third day, or will you be left in the darkness of the Tribulation?**

Chapter 6 – Subtracting Seven Years: The Tribulation Factor

Why 2032 Minus 7 Brings Us to 2025

The Prophetic Necessity of the Final Countdown

Why Subtract Seven Years?

If Hosea's prophecy sets the visible return of Christ in **AD 2032**, why do we speak of the Rapture happening in **2025**? The answer is simple: Scripture tells us that before Christ's reign begins, there will be a **seven-year Tribulation**.

This is not speculation. Daniel 9:27 lays out the final "week" — a period of seven years when the Antichrist will confirm a covenant, desecrate the Temple, and bring desolation until Christ destroys him at His coming. Revelation 11–13 also confirms this period, describing 1,260 days, 42 months, and "a time, times, and half a time," all pointing to halves of a seven-year span.

Therefore, if the visible return of Christ is in 2032, the Tribulation must begin in 2025. The Rapture happens before it, bringing the Church out of the way before wrath falls (1 Thessalonians 1:10). That is why the Rapture falls not in 2032 but in September 2025.

Daniel's 70th Week

The Tribulation is not just a random span of suffering. It is the **70th week of Daniel's prophecy** (Daniel 9:24–27).

- **Weeks 1–69**: Fulfilled in Israel's history, leading up to Christ's first coming.
- **Gap**: The Church Age, lasting nearly 2,000 years.
- **Week 70**: Still unfulfilled, reserved for the time of the end.

Daniel 9:27 says: *"He shall confirm a covenant with many for one week; but in the middle of the week he shall bring an end to sacrifice and offering."* This final week of seven years is what Revelation expands into the judgments of seals, trumpets, and bowls.

Without subtracting these seven years, Hosea's timeline would not align with Daniel's prophecy. Both must fit together like puzzle pieces.

The Purpose of the Tribulation

Why does God allow this final seven years? The Bible gives us three purposes:

1. **To Judge the Nations**
    - Revelation 6–16 describes God's wrath poured out on the unbelieving world.

   - This is the time of "the day of the Lord" (Isaiah 13:6–11; 1 Thessalonians 5:2–3).

2. **To Purify Israel**
   - Jeremiah 30:7 calls it "the time of Jacob's trouble."
   - Zechariah 13:9 says a remnant of Israel will be refined like silver and tested like gold.
   - By the end, "all Israel will be saved" (Romans 11:26).

3. **To Finish the Story**
   - Every prophecy about Antichrist, false worship, the mark of the beast, and global deception comes to pass.
   - Evil reaches its climax before Christ crushes it forever.

The Tribulation is both judgment and mercy. Judgment on sin. Mercy on those who repent in the last hour.

Why 2025 and Not Later?

If Christ's visible return is in 2032, subtracting seven years gives us 2025. This is where Hosea and Daniel overlap. But there's more:

- **Brother Joshua's testimony:** Jesus appeared to him and said the Rapture would take place September 23–25, 2025.
- **The Feast of Trumpets:** The Rapture aligns with this feast, which always falls in September.

- **The countdown of Ecclesiastes:** The 28th season ends in June 2025, the start of the time of peace. Yet that peace only arrives after the Rapture removes the Church.

All prophetic roads converge on September 2025. This is not guesswork — it is God's appointed time.

The Pattern of Seven

The number seven is God's prophetic signature.

- Seven days of creation, ending in rest.
- Seven years of famine in Egypt (Genesis 41).
- Seven cycles of seven in Israel's calendar (Leviticus 25).
- Seven seals, trumpets, and bowls in Revelation.

The seven-year Tribulation is not an accident. It is the final cycle, the last countdown, the "week" that must be completed before Christ returns.

The Rapture Before Wrath

Some ask: Will the Church endure part of the Tribulation? Scripture is clear: **the Church is not appointed to wrath** (1 Thessalonians 5:9).

- Revelation 3:10 – *"I will keep you from the hour of trial which shall come upon the whole world."*
- Luke 21:36 – *"Pray that you may be counted worthy to escape all these things."*

- 1 Thessalonians 4:16–17 – The Rapture itself, the catching away before wrath begins.

This is why the Rapture must precede the Tribulation. We are removed so God can finish His plan with Israel and the nations.

What Happens After the Rapture

When the Rapture occurs in September 2025, the world will be thrown into chaos. Millions vanish, children disappear, and the global economy collapses. Out of this chaos, the Antichrist rises with false peace.

The seven years will unfold in two halves:

1. **First 3½ Years (False Peace)**
    - Covenant confirmed with Israel.
    - Temple worship restored.
    - Antichrist appears as a man of peace.
2. **Last 3½ Years (Great Tribulation)**
    - Antichrist breaks the covenant.
    - The abomination of desolation set up in the Temple.
    - Global persecution, mark of the beast, wrath of God poured out.

Then, at the end of 2032, Christ returns with His saints to defeat the Antichrist and begin His reign.

The Urgency of the Countdown

If the Rapture is in 2025, we are only days away. This is why prophecy is urgent. Hosea's two days end in AD 2032, but subtracting seven years shows that the next event — the Rapture — comes sooner than most expect.

Every second is precious. Every soul matters. Every warning must be given.

What This Means for Believers

For believers, the Tribulation factor changes everything.

- **We don't live as if we have seven more years.** We live as if we have only days.
- **We don't ignore prophecy.** We use it to stir our hearts with urgency.
- **We don't hide in fear.** We prepare with hope, because deliverance is near.

Understanding the Tribulation factor means understanding that God's clock is about to strike. The trumpet is next.

What This Means for the World

For the unbelieving world, the Tribulation will be a nightmare.

- Global wars, famine, and death (Revelation 6).
- A one-world system of government and religion (Revelation 13).

- The mark of the beast, without which no one can buy or sell.
- The greatest deception in human history.

This is why the Rapture is God's mercy. He is removing His people before the storm.

Key Takeaways

1. Hosea's two days end in 2032.
2. Subtracting seven years for the Tribulation brings us to 2025.
3. Daniel's 70th week and Revelation's prophecies confirm this.
4. The Rapture must happen before wrath falls.
5. The countdown is almost over — the trumpet is near.

Closing Reflection

The Tribulation is not an abstract idea. It is the final seven years of history as we know it. It is the storm before the sunrise, the night before the dawn.

By subtracting seven years from AD 2032, we see that the Rapture must occur in 2025. Hosea's prophecy, Daniel's vision, Revelation's warnings, and the testimony of Brother Joshua all align.

The question is not whether this will happen — the question is whether you will be ready. The trumpet is about to sound. Will you rise to meet Christ in the air, or will you be left behind to endure the Tribulation?

Chapter 7 – The Feast of Trumpets and the Rapture Connection

Why God Chose the Feast of Trumpets for the Rapture

How Brother Joshua's Prophecy Confirms the Appointed Day

God's Appointed Times

The Bible is full of **appointed times**. In Leviticus 23, God commanded Israel to keep seven feasts. These were not just holidays — they were prophetic markers of His plan.

- The spring feasts (Passover, Unleavened Bread, Firstfruits, Pentecost) were fulfilled in Christ's death, burial, resurrection, and the coming of the Spirit.
- The fall feasts (Trumpets, Atonement, Tabernacles) remain prophetic, pointing to end-time events and the reign of Messiah.

The Feast of Trumpets — also called Rosh Hashanah — has long been seen as the prophetic picture of the Rapture. Its themes of sounding the trumpet, announcing the King, and calling God's people together perfectly align with Paul's description of the Rapture in 1 Thessalonians 4:16–17.

The Feast of Trumpets in 2025

To understand why September 23–24, 2025 is the day, we must look at the actual Jewish calendar for that year.

- The **new moon of Tishri** marks the start of the feast. In 2025, this happens on **the evening of Sunday, September 21**.
- By Jewish reckoning, the feast officially begins at **sundown September 22** in Israel.
- The feast lasts for **two days**. Therefore, the **second day is September 23**, when most of the world will still be within that appointed season.

This means the most prophetically fitting day for the Rapture is **September 23, 2025**, the second day of the Feast of Trumpets.

Brother Joshua's Testimony

In 2018, Jesus appeared directly to Brother Joshua from Africa. He was not dreaming. He was not in a vision. He was awake. Jesus told him plainly that the Rapture would happen on **September 23–24, 2025**.

This was exactly **seven years in advance** — just as Noah was given **seven days of warning** before the flood (Genesis 7:4). God gave His servant a specific warning so that His people would not be caught off guard.

At first, many dismissed it. They said, "No man knows the day or hour." But when compared to the Feast of Trumpets calendar and Hosea's prophecy of two days, the timing lines up with absolute precision.

Why the Feast of Trumpets Fits the Rapture

The Feast of Trumpets is unique among the feasts.

- **The Last Trumpet:** Paul said the Rapture happens "at the last trumpet" (1 Corinthians 15:52). The feast is marked by a series of trumpet blasts.
- **The Day No Man Knows:** Because the feast begins at the sighting of the new moon, it is traditionally called "the day and hour no man knows." This is exactly what Jesus said about His coming (Matthew 24:36).
- **The Gathering:** Trumpets were used in Israel to gather the assembly (Numbers 10:2). The Rapture is the ultimate gathering of God's people.
- **The Coronation of the King:** Jewish tradition connects the feast with the crowning of kings. At the Rapture, Christ is revealed as the returning King.

Every theme of the Feast of Trumpets points to the Rapture. It is no wonder that God revealed to Brother Joshua that this would be the appointed time.

The Prophetic Calendar Alignment

Let's review the prophetic alignment:

1. **AD 32:** Resurrection of Christ. Hosea's "two days" begin.
2. **AD 2032:** Two thousand years later — the visible return of Christ.
3. **Subtract 7 years:** Brings us to 2025 — the Tribulation must begin.
4. **Feast of Trumpets, 2025:** September 23–24 aligns perfectly.
5. **Brother Joshua's testimony:** Jesus confirmed this exact date in 2018.

This is not guesswork. It is prophecy, Scripture, and direct revelation converging on one moment in time.

The Second Day of the Feast

Why does the Rapture fall on the **second day**?

Because in Jewish reckoning, the feast begins at the first sight of the new moon. In 2025, that is the evening of September 22 in Israel. The **23rd becomes the second day**, which carries prophetic significance:

- It matches Hosea's prophecy of "after two days."
- It matches the idea of "confirmation" — the first day declares, the second day establishes.
- It matches the global timeline — when Israel is in the 23rd, most of the world is still in daylight hours.

This shows God's precision. The second day of the feast — September 23 — is the appointed moment.

Seven Years of Warning

God always warns His people. He warned Noah seven days before the flood. He warned Israel through the prophets before judgment fell. And He has now given His Church seven years' warning through Brother Joshua.

- In 2018, Jesus appeared and gave the date.
- Seven years later, in 2025, the event will happen.
- This fits God's pattern of mercy and preparation.

Those who mock the warning will be left behind. Those who heed it will be ready to meet the Lord in the air.

What Will Happen at the Feast

When the trumpet sounds, here is what Scripture says will happen:

- **The Dead in Christ will rise first** (1 Thessalonians 4:16). Every believer who has died since the resurrection will be raised with a glorified body.
- **We who are alive will be caught up** (1 Thessalonians 4:17). Believers alive on earth will instantly be transformed.
- **We will meet the Lord in the air.** This is the great gathering, the marriage supper of the Lamb about to begin.
- **The world will be thrown into chaos.** Millions vanish, children disappear, economies collapse, and fear fills the nations.

The trumpet of God will fulfill the Feast of Trumpets on that very day.

Why This Matters Now

If September 23, 2025 is the day, we have less than two weeks left. The urgency could not be greater.

- Do not wait to repent.
- Do not assume you will have another chance.
- Do not mock prophecy or delay obedience.

This is the moment to be ready.

Key Takeaways

1. The Feast of Trumpets is the prophetic picture of the Rapture.
2. In 2025, the feast begins at sundown September 22 and continues into September 23.
3. The second day of the feast — September 23 — is the appointed day.
4. Brother Joshua's testimony matches this exact date.
5. The Rapture will fulfill the feast with perfect precision.

Closing Reflection

The Feast of Trumpets is no longer just a shadow. In 2025, it will become reality. The trumpet will sound, the dead will rise, and the Church will be caught up to meet the Lord.

Jesus has confirmed this through His Word, through the prophetic calendar, and through direct revelation to His servant, Brother Joshua. The second day of the feast — September 23, 2025 — is the appointed time.

The warning has been given. The seven years are almost complete. The question is not whether this will happen — the question is whether you will be ready.

Chapter 8 – What Will Happen When Millions Vanish

The World's Most Shocking Day

Why Life Will Never Return to Normal

The Day That Changes Everything

The Rapture will not be a quiet event. It will not be hidden in a corner. It will be the most shocking, visible, undeniable moment in world history. In a single instant, millions of believers and all children under the age of accountability will vanish.

This will not happen gradually. It will be sudden. Families will wake up to discover their children gone. Husbands will reach for wives who are no longer there. Friends will search for neighbors who disappeared without warning. The event will shake every nation, every city, every family.

Paul described it clearly in 1 Thessalonians 4:16–17: *"For the Lord Himself will descend from heaven with a shout, with the voice of an archangel, and with the trumpet of God. And the dead in Christ will rise first. Then we who are alive and remain shall be caught up together with them in the clouds to meet the Lord in the air. And thus we shall always be with the Lord."*

What Paul foresaw is about to happen.

The Chaos of a Vanishing World

The moment the Rapture happens, society will collapse into chaos.

- **Planes will fall from the sky.** Pilots who are believers will vanish mid-flight, causing instant crashes.
- **Cars will collide everywhere.** Millions of drivers will disappear while vehicles are in motion.
- **Workplaces will be emptied.** Factories, hospitals, schools, and offices will lose staff without explanation.
- **Families will be devastated.** Parents will lose children, children will lose parents, spouses will lose partners.

Luke 17:34–35 says, *"I tell you, in that night there will be two men in one bed: the one will be taken and the other will be left. Two women will be grinding together: the one will be taken and the other left."*

Jesus' words describe the separation and devastation perfectly.

The Global Impact

This will not be a local event. It will affect every nation on earth simultaneously.

- Economies will collapse overnight.

- Governments will lose leaders and soldiers.
- Communication systems will break down.
- Stock markets will crash permanently.
- International trade will halt.

The Rapture will cripple the infrastructure of the modern world. It will mark the beginning of the most unstable period in human history.

The Disappearance of Children

Perhaps the most painful shock will be the disappearance of all children under the age of accountability. From nurseries to schools, from homes to playgrounds, every child will vanish in an instant.

Mothers will collapse in anguish. Fathers will search in vain. Nations will mourn. This single fact alone will devastate humanity in a way never seen before.

Jesus said in Matthew 19:14: *"Let the little children come to Me, and do not forbid them; for of such is the kingdom of heaven."* On that day, every child will go to be with Him.

No Return to Normal

Some may believe that the world will recover, that governments will stabilize, and life will go on. But Scripture says otherwise.

Jesus said in Matthew 24:21: *"For then there will be great tribulation, such as has not been since the beginning of the world until this time, no, nor ever shall be."*

After the Rapture, there will be no return to normal. 2026 will not be business as usual. It will be a world scarred by loss, fear, and the beginning of judgment.

The Rise of False Explanations

The world will not admit that the Rapture was God's doing. Leaders will rush to invent explanations.

- Aliens.
- Secret government projects.
- Spontaneous evolutionary change.
- Mass hysteria.

2 Thessalonians 2:11 warns: *"And for this reason God will send them strong delusion, that they should believe the lie."* The Antichrist will use this moment to rise in power, promising answers and solutions.

The Shaking of Every Foundation

The Rapture will shake the world at every level:

1. **Social:** Families torn apart by missing loved ones.
2. **Political:** Governments collapsing without leaders.
3. **Economic:** Markets ruined by sudden loss of workers and consumers.
4. **Religious:** False systems exposed as powerless, while true prophecy is vindicated.

5. **Spiritual:** The age of grace ending, and the age of wrath beginning.

The event will mark a permanent shift. Nothing will ever be the same again.

Why This Warning Matters

If you are reading this before the Rapture, the warning is simple: you cannot afford to miss it. Do not delay repentance. Do not assume you will have another chance.

If you are reading this after the Rapture, know that what happened was not random. It was God's appointed time. But now, you must endure the Tribulation, reject the mark of the beast, and cling to Christ until the end.

Key Takeaways

- The Rapture will remove millions of believers and all children in a single moment.
- The world will plunge into chaos — planes, cars, governments, economies, and families shattered.
- False explanations will arise, but Scripture already told us the truth.
- Life will never return to normal. The Tribulation begins immediately.
- This is why the warning must be taken seriously today.

Closing Reflection

The Rapture is not just a theological idea. It is a global crisis. It is the day when millions vanish, children are taken, and the world collapses into chaos.

2026 will not be business as usual. It will be the dawn of Tribulation, the rise of Antichrist, and the beginning of judgment.

But for those who are ready, the Rapture is hope. It is joy. It is the moment we meet the Lord in the air.

The trumpet is about to sound. The only question is: **Will you be taken, or left behind when millions vanish?**

Chapter 9 – Living in the Final Hours Before the Trumpet

The Urgency of Hosea's Prophecy

Why Every Choice Matters in the Last Moments

The Final Countdown

We are not living in ordinary times. Hosea's prophecy of two days — two thousand years — is nearly complete. The calendar is closing, and the trumpet is about to sound.

Paul warned us in Romans 13:11: *"Knowing the time, that now it is high time to awake out of sleep; for now our salvation is nearer than when we first believed."* Every sign points to this reality: we are in the **final hours of the second day**.

If you are reading this before the Rapture, you have only a brief window left. These are the last minutes on God's prophetic clock.

Why Readiness Matters

Jesus gave repeated warnings about readiness. *"Therefore you also be ready, for the Son of Man is coming at an hour you do not expect"* (Matthew 24:44). The trumpet will not give advance notice. It will sound suddenly, and in an instant everything will change.

Readiness is not about religion or ritual. It is about relationship with Christ. It means your sins are forgiven, your heart is surrendered, and your life belongs to Him. Anything less is dangerous self-deception.

The Call to Repentance

In these last hours, repentance is not optional. Jesus began His ministry with the words: *"Repent, for the kingdom of heaven is at hand"* (Matthew 4:17). That same message is the final call before the trumpet.

Repentance means more than saying "sorry." It means turning from sin and walking in obedience. It means laying down pride, bitterness, lust, greed, and every hidden idol. It means surrendering your heart fully to Christ.

Without repentance, you cannot be ready. With repentance, you will hear the trumpet with joy.

Living With Eternity in View

Every decision matters more in the final hours. How you spend your time, where you invest your energy, what you cling to — all of it carries eternal weight.

- Do you choose Christ over comfort?
- Do you prioritize prayer over distraction?

- Do you love others with sacrificial love?
- Do you live with eternity as your focus?

Colossians 3:2 tells us: *"Set your mind on things above, not on things on the earth."* When eternity fills your vision, you will not waste the final hours.

The Signs Around Us

Jesus gave clear signs of the end: wars, famines, earthquakes, lawlessness, and deception (Matthew 24). Paul spoke of perilous times when people would be lovers of themselves, proud, unholy, and lovers of pleasure rather than lovers of God (2 Timothy 3).

Look around. Every sign is here. The world is unraveling exactly as prophecy said it would. This is not coincidence — it is confirmation. The trumpet is closer than ever.

Clinging to Faith, Love, and Obedience

In the final hours, three things must anchor your life:

1. **Faith** – Trusting God even when fear rises. Believing His promises are true.
2. **Love** – Choosing compassion, forgiveness, and sacrifice in a world of selfishness.
3. **Obedience** – Walking in holiness, not compromise. Doing what God says, no matter the cost.

1 Corinthians 13:13 reminds us: *"And now abide faith, hope, love, these three; but the greatest of these is love."* But in these last hours, obedience shows whether our faith and love are real.

The Danger of Delay

The greatest mistake in these final hours is delay. Some say, "I will repent tomorrow. I will surrender later." But tomorrow is not guaranteed.

Proverbs 27:1 warns: *"Do not boast about tomorrow, for you do not know what a day may bring forth."* When the trumpet sounds, the door will shut — just as it did in Noah's day. Delay now means regret forever.

How to Live in the Final Hours

Here are practical steps to live ready in the last moments before the trumpet:

- **Stay awake spiritually.** Do not let distraction or sin lull you to sleep.
- **Pray daily.** Build intimacy with God through constant communion.
- **Be in the Word.** Let Scripture cleanse and strengthen your mind.
- **Share the gospel.** Warn others urgently while there is still time.
- **Walk in holiness.** Reject compromise and live as Christ's representative.

These are not suggestions. They are survival instructions for the final hours.

The Weight of Eternity

Every choice you make now echoes into eternity. Jesus said in Revelation 22:12: *"Behold, I am coming quickly, and My reward is with Me, to give to every one according to his work."*

Will your choices show you were ready, faithful, and surrendered? Or will they reveal compromise and unbelief? The weight of eternity rests on how you live in these last hours.

Key Takeaways

- We are living in the final hours before the trumpet.
- Hosea's prophecy of two days is nearly complete.
- Readiness means repentance, faith, love, and obedience.
- Delay is dangerous — the door will soon shut.
- Every decision now carries eternal weight.

Closing Reflection

The trumpet is about to sound. Hosea's two days are almost finished. We are living in the final hours before Christ gathers His people.

Every choice you make now matters. Eternity is at stake. The window is almost closed, and God's final warning has been given.

The question is simple: **Will you be ready when the trumpet sounds, or will you be caught unprepared in the final hours?**

Chapter 10 – After the Rapture: A Message to the Left Behind

The World You Now Face

How to Survive the Tribulation and Find Eternal Hope

The Shocking Reality

If you are reading these words after the Rapture, then what the Bible prophesied has already come to pass. Millions of believers, along with all the children of the world, have vanished in an instant. Planes fell from the sky, cars crashed into one another, families were torn apart, and governments collapsed under the weight of sudden chaos.

This was not an accident. It was not an alien invasion. It was not a global experiment gone wrong. It was exactly what Jesus promised: *"I will come again and receive you to Myself; that where I am, there you may be also"* (John 14:3). The disappearance you have just witnessed is the **Rapture of the Church**.

If you were left behind, it means you were not ready. But it does not mean all hope is lost.

The Lies of the World

The world will rush to explain away what has happened. Leaders, scientists, and media will push narratives designed to soothe fear and control the masses.

- Some will say it was **aliens** removing humanity for an evolutionary leap.
- Others will claim it was a **government experiment** gone wrong.
- Still others will insist it was a **natural cosmic disaster**.

But all of these are lies. Paul warned in 2 Thessalonians 2:11 that God would allow a "strong delusion" so that people would believe the lie. The truth is simple: Jesus has taken His people. The Church has been removed.

Do not believe the lies. Cling to the truth of God's Word.

Entering the Tribulation

What lies ahead of you now is the seven-year Tribulation. Daniel 9:27 calls it the final "week" of years — a covenant confirmed and then broken, leading to desolation. Revelation 6–19 describes it in detail: war, famine, plagues, earthquakes, persecution, and global deception.

The Antichrist will rise to power, promising peace and stability in the midst of chaos. He will unite governments, economies, and religions under his rule. For the first 3½ years, he will appear as a savior. But then he will reveal his true nature, desecrate the rebuilt Temple in Jerusalem, and demand worship as God.

This will begin the "Great Tribulation" — the second half of the seven years — when persecution and judgment will reach their peak.

The Mark of the Beast

Revelation 13 describes the coming system: *"He causes all, both small and great, rich and poor, free and slave, to receive a mark on their right hand or on their foreheads, and that no one may buy or sell except one who has the mark or the name of the beast, or the number of his name."*

This mark will be presented as the solution to economic collapse. Without it, you will not be able to buy food, hold a job, or participate in society. But taking it will seal your fate eternally. Revelation 14:11 warns that those who receive the mark will face eternal torment.

You must refuse the mark. Even if it costs you your life, your soul will be saved.

The Cost of Faith

Choosing Christ in the Tribulation will not be easy. It will cost you everything. Revelation 6:9 describes the martyrs who are slain for the Word of God and their testimony. Revelation 12:11 says, *"They overcame him by the blood of the Lamb and by the word of their testimony, and they did not love their lives to the death."*

You may lose your freedom. You may lose your family. You may lose your life. But you will gain eternal life with Christ. The temporary suffering of these seven years cannot compare to the eternal joy that awaits you.

Finding Strength in Scripture

Even though the Church has been taken, the Word of God remains. Cling to it. Read it daily. Memorize it. Hide it in your heart.

Key passages for you now:

- **Revelation 6–19** – The events of the Tribulation.
- **Matthew 24–25** – Jesus' warnings about the end times.
- **Daniel 9–12** – Prophecies about the final week.
- **Psalm 91** – God's promise of protection for those who trust Him.

The Bible will be your guide, your comfort, and your strength in these dark days.

What You Must Do Now

If you were left behind, here are the steps you must take immediately:

1. **Repent** – Turn to Christ in full surrender. Confess your sins and trust in His sacrifice.
2. **Reject the Mark** – No matter what, do not accept the system of the Antichrist.
3. **Prepare to Endure** – Be ready for persecution, hardship, and even death.
4. **Seek Other Believers** – Find those who also refuse the mark. Encourage one another.

5. **Hold Fast to Hope** – Remember, this period will last only seven years. Christ will return visibly to reign.

The Comfort of God's Promise

Even in these darkest days, God has not abandoned you. Revelation 7:14 describes a great multitude who come out of the Tribulation, clothed in white robes, having washed them in the blood of the Lamb.

You can be among them. If you hold fast, if you endure to the end, if you refuse to bow to the Antichrist, you will be saved. Jesus' promise is still true: *"Be faithful until death, and I will give you the crown of life"* (Revelation 2:10).

Key Takeaways

- The Rapture has happened. Millions are gone.
- Do not believe the lies of the world. This was Jesus fulfilling His promise.
- You are now in the Tribulation — seven years of judgment.
- The Antichrist will rise with false peace and demand the mark of the beast.
- Refuse the mark, endure persecution, and cling to Christ for eternal life.

Closing Reflection

If you are reading this after the Rapture, you are living in the most terrifying period of human history. But you are also living in the final countdown to Christ's visible return.

The chaos you see is not the end — it is the beginning of the end. The Tribulation will last seven years, and then Jesus will return to reign. If you endure, you will share in His victory.

Do not take the mark. Do not deny Christ. Repent, believe, and hold fast. Eternal life is still within reach, but only if you remain faithful in the darkest hour.

The trumpet has sounded, the Church is gone, but hope is not lost. The choice before you is clear: **Follow Christ and endure, or follow the beast and perish. The decision is yours.**

Chapter 11 – Life After the Rapture: The World in Chaos

What Happens the Day After Millions Vanish

How the World Will Collapse Into Tribulation

The Shocking Moment

In a single instant, millions will disappear. The trumpet will sound, the dead in Christ will rise, and living believers will be caught up to meet the Lord in the air (1 Thessalonians 4:16–17). But for those left behind, the world will plunge into chaos.

Imagine the scenes. Airplanes crashing because pilots vanish. Cars colliding because drivers are gone. Families screaming because children under the age of accountability disappear from every home. Governments scrambling because leaders, soldiers, and workers vanish. This is not fiction — it is the next event on God's calendar.

The Rapture is the beginning of the Tribulation. It is the dividing line between mercy and judgment, between grace and wrath.

Global Panic

The day after the Rapture, nothing will be the same.

- Hospitals will overflow with casualties from sudden accidents.
- Stock markets will collapse as millions of jobs vanish overnight.
- Entire industries will break down without workers.
- Nations will declare martial law to control the panic.
- Rumors will spread — aliens, conspiracies, government experiments.

Jesus said, *"Men's hearts failing them from fear, and the expectation of those things which are coming on the earth"* (Luke 21:26). The world will not recover from the shock.

The Loss of the Children

Perhaps the most devastating blow will be the loss of the children. Every child below the age of accountability — whether 6, 7, or 8 years old — will be instantly taken to be with the Lord.

Parents will wail in agony. Hospitals will be emptied of newborns. Schools and nurseries will be left desolate. Governments will not know how to explain it.

For many, this will be the breaking point. Families will never be the same. Whole nations will reel under the grief.

The Great Deception

In the midst of this chaos, leaders will scramble for explanations. The Antichrist will rise with smooth words and deceptive answers.

- He may say aliens took humanity into a "new age."
- He may claim evolution demanded a leap forward.
- He may promise peace and safety if the world unites.

Paul warned in 2 Thessalonians 2:11 that *"God will send them strong delusion, that they should believe the lie."* Those who rejected the truth before the Rapture will be deceived after it.

The Worldwide EMP

According to many testimonies, the Rapture will trigger a catastrophic event in the natural world as well. All electronics will burn out in a massive worldwide EMP (electromagnetic pulse).

- Phones will stop working.
- Cars and planes will fail.
- The internet will collapse forever.
- Governments will lose control of their systems.

In a single day, humanity will be thrown back to a pre-technological age. This will strip away the distractions of sin but also plunge the world into unimaginable struggle.

The Rise of the Beast

Revelation 13 describes the coming Antichrist — a beast with authority over every tribe, tongue, and nation. After the Rapture, he will step forward as a man of peace. He will promise solutions to the chaos. He will unite governments, religions, and economies.

But his peace will be false. Halfway through the seven years, he will reveal his true nature, demand worship, and unleash persecution on all who refuse to take his mark.

The chaos of the Rapture will be his platform for power.

Economic Collapse

Without millions of workers, without technology, and without stability, the global economy will collapse.

- Food supplies will dwindle.
- Trade routes will break down.
- Cash will be useless in many places.
- A new system of buying and selling will be required — the mark of the beast (Revelation 13:16–17).

The economy will never recover. What begins as financial panic will end as economic slavery under Antichrist.

Religious Confusion

After the Rapture, many churches will be empty — because the true believers are gone. But many religious leaders who never truly knew

Christ will still be here. They will join the deception, forming a one-world religion.

Revelation 17 calls this the "great harlot" — a false religious system that partners with political power. It will claim to speak for God but will lead people straight into destruction.

Only those who turn to Christ in the Tribulation will resist. Many will be martyred for their faith.

Violence and War

As nations collapse, violence will spread. Revelation 6 describes the second horseman of the apocalypse — war. Peace will be taken from the earth, and people will kill one another.

- Civil wars will erupt in nations torn by panic.
- International wars will break out over resources.
- Armies will rise to fight for dominance.

The chaos after the Rapture will quickly escalate into global bloodshed.

The Three Days of Darkness

Many prophetic voices warn that when the Rapture happens, three days of supernatural darkness will cover the earth. During this time, demonic forces will be unleashed to kill, torment, and terrify.

- Windows must be covered.
- No one should go outside.

- Only the light of candles or oil lamps will work.

This will be God's judgment, a foreshadowing of the plagues of Egypt, and a sign that the age of mercy is over.

What Believers Must Do Now

If you are reading this before the Rapture, the warning is clear: do not delay. Repent now. Turn fully to Christ. Do not assume you can survive the chaos after the Rapture.

If you are reading this after the Rapture, there is still hope. You must repent, refuse the mark of the beast, and endure until the end. It will cost you everything, but eternal life is worth it.

Key Takeaways

1. The Rapture will instantly throw the world into chaos.
2. Children will vanish, families will be devastated, and economies will collapse.
3. Electronics will fail, leaving the world permanently crippled.
4. The Antichrist will rise, bringing false peace and global control.
5. Only those who repent after the Rapture will be saved — but at great cost.

Reflection Questions

- Do I grasp how devastating the world will be the day after the Rapture?
- Have I shared this warning with those I love before it is too late?
- If I were left behind, what choice would I make when confronted with the mark of the beast?
- Am I living now as if I believe the trumpet is about to sound?

Closing Reflection

Life after the Rapture will not be business as usual. It will be chaos, terror, and judgment. The loss of children, the collapse of nations, and the rise of Antichrist will make 2026 unrecognizable.

But for those who belong to Christ, the Rapture is not terror — it is hope. We will escape the wrath to come and reign with Him forever.

The question is simple: **Will you be gone in the Rapture, or left behind in the chaos?**

Chapter 12 – The Bible's Prophecies Always Come True

Why History Confirms Every Word of Scripture

Living with Confidence in God's Perfect Record

The Nature of Prophecy

Prophecy is one of the greatest proofs that the Bible is truly the Word of God. No other book in history dares to predict the future with specific detail thousands of years in advance. Yet the Scriptures do this repeatedly.

Isaiah 46:9–10 records God's own words: *"I am God, and there is no other; I am God, and there is none like Me, declaring the end from the beginning, and from ancient times things that are not yet done."* Prophecy is God's signature. It shows that He alone controls time and history.

When we see prophecy fulfilled, it is not coincidence. It is confirmation that the Author of history is also the Author of Scripture. That means every prophecy yet to come will be fulfilled just as surely as those already past.

Prophecies of the Messiah

The clearest example is the life of Jesus Christ. The Old Testament contained hundreds of prophecies about the Messiah, written centuries before His birth. Each one came true with perfect accuracy.

- **Born in Bethlehem** – Micah 5:2 said, *"But you, Bethlehem Ephrathah... out of you shall come forth to Me the One to be Ruler in Israel."* Fulfilled in Matthew 2:1.
- **Born of a virgin** – Isaiah 7:14 foretold, *"Behold, the virgin shall conceive and bear a Son, and shall call His name Immanuel."* Fulfilled in Luke 1:27–35.
- **Betrayed for thirty pieces of silver** – Zechariah 11:12–13 declared the exact amount. Fulfilled in Matthew 26:15.
- **Pierced hands and feet** – Psalm 22:16 described crucifixion centuries before it was invented. Fulfilled in John 19:18.
- **Buried in a rich man's tomb** – Isaiah 53:9 said the Suffering Servant would be with the rich in His death. Fulfilled in Matthew 27:57–60.

These are not vague predictions. They are specific details written hundreds of years before Christ came. And all were fulfilled in His first coming.

Prophecies of Israel

God's dealings with Israel provide another undeniable proof. The rise, fall, exile, and regathering of Israel were all foretold long before they happened.

- **Exile to Babylon** – Jeremiah 25:11–12 said Judah would serve the king of Babylon for seventy years. Fulfilled from 586–516 BC.

- **Return from exile** – Isaiah 44:28 named King Cyrus by name 150 years before he was born, predicting he would allow Jerusalem to be rebuilt. Fulfilled in Ezra 1:1–4.

- **Scattering of Israel** – Deuteronomy 28:64 warned that Israel would be scattered among all nations. Fulfilled after AD 70 when Rome destroyed Jerusalem.

- **Regathering in the last days** – Ezekiel 37 foresaw dry bones coming to life as the nation of Israel restored. Fulfilled in 1948 when Israel was reborn.

Every one of these events is recorded in history. Israel's story follows prophecy like a script written in advance.

Prophecies of Nations

God also foretold the destinies of nations.

- **Nineveh's fall** – Nahum prophesied its destruction (Nahum 3:7). Fulfilled in 612 BC.

- **Babylon's desolation** – Isaiah 13:19–20 said Babylon would never be inhabited. Today it remains in ruins.

- **Rise of Persia and Greece** – Daniel 8 predicted a ram (Persia) and a goat (Greece) centuries before Alexander the Great.

History is the record of prophecy fulfilled. Nations rise and fall exactly as God declared.

The Accuracy of Timing

Not only are events predicted, but sometimes even the timing is given. Daniel's prophecy of the "seventy weeks" (Daniel 9:24–26) pinpointed the exact timing of Messiah's first coming. From the decree to rebuild Jerusalem until the arrival of Messiah was predicted as 483 years. When the years are counted precisely, it lands on the time of Jesus' triumphal entry into Jerusalem.

This shows prophecy is not symbolic guesswork. It is mathematically precise. The same God who counted the hairs on our head also counts the days of history.

Why This Matters for Today

If every prophecy in the past has come true, what does that mean for the ones still ahead? It means they will be fulfilled exactly the same way.

Jesus promised to return (John 14:3). Paul described the Rapture (1 Thessalonians 4:16–17). John recorded visions of the Tribulation, the rise of the Antichrist, and the return of Christ (Revelation 6–19). None of these are speculative ideas. They are certain realities.

Just as Bethlehem was not a metaphor, the Rapture is not a metaphor. Just as Israel's exile was literal, the Tribulation will be literal. Just as

Jesus' first coming happened exactly as foretold, His second coming will also happen exactly as written.

The Danger of Scoffing

Peter warned in 2 Peter 3:3–4: *"Scoffers will come in the last days, walking according to their own lusts, and saying, 'Where is the promise of His coming?'"* Scoffing is one of the last-day signs. Many dismiss prophecy as outdated or irrelevant. Yet that very attitude was itself predicted.

History shows that scoffers have always been proven wrong. In Noah's day, people mocked until the rain came. In Jeremiah's day, they ignored the warnings until Babylon arrived. Today, people laugh at the idea of the Rapture and Christ's return. But when prophecy is fulfilled, scoffing will not stop it.

Living with Confidence

For believers, prophecy is not meant to terrify but to reassure. Jesus said in John 13:19, *"Now I tell you before it comes, that when it does come to pass, you may believe that I am He."* Prophecy builds faith. When we see fulfilled prophecy, it proves again that God's Word is true.

This means we can trust His promises for the future. If He said He will come for His people, He will. If He said He will establish His Kingdom, He will. If He said He will judge sin, He will.

We do not need to fear uncertainty. The future is already written by the Author of history.

Key Takeaways

- Prophecy is God's proof that He controls history.
- Past prophecies about Messiah, Israel, and nations have been fulfilled with perfect accuracy.
- This proves future prophecies will also be fulfilled exactly as written.
- Scoffers will deny it, but prophecy always comes true.
- Believers can live with confidence because God's Word has never failed.

Closing Challenge

The Bible's record is perfect. Every word God has spoken has come to pass, and every word still unfulfilled will happen in His appointed time. The prophecies about the last days are not warnings we can ignore; they are promises we must prepare for.

History proves it. Scripture confirms it. The Rapture is certain. The Tribulation is certain. The return of Christ is certain. The only question left is this: **Will you be ready when God fulfills His next prophecy?**

Other Books By the *Team Success Network* - In The "Team Success" Series Include:

Book 1 - Kingdom of Heaven – Team Success Network

Book 2 - Building Duplicatable "Mutual Success Team" Business Projects

Book 3 - Team Success Network: Leadership, Development, Summits, & Discipleship

Book 4 - AI Tools - Team Success Network - Enhancing Mutual Success Teams Using AI Tools

Book 5 - Team Success Network: Global Organization & Resources

Book 6 - 200+ Business Project Ideas – For Mutual Success Teams

Book 7 - The FAITH HEALING TRAININGS - Learn Healing As a Skill

Book 8 - Using Christian Decks as Your First "Mutual Success Project"

Meet the Author – Elijah J Stone

Founder of the Team Success Network

Hi, I'm Elijah. I wrote this book because I believe God is calling the Church into a new era—where we don't just gather, we build. I'm not a celebrity, a pastor of a mega church, or a spiritual expert. I'm someone like you—who saw the need and heard the call.

The Team Success Network is not just a concept. It's a movement of real believers working together to bring God's Kingdom into real life—through unity, purpose, and mutual success. I hope this book encourages and equips you to step into your role.

If this vision speaks to your heart, I'd love to hear from you.

Email me personally: elijah@teamsuccessnetwork.com

Let's keep building—together.

Stay Connected – Your Next Step Starts Now

You've made it through this book—but that doesn't mean the journey is over. In fact, it may just be beginning.

The Team Success Network was created for people like you—believers who are ready to live differently, work together, and take action that transforms lives. If something in these pages sparked a new idea, birthed a desire to join or lead a team, or helped you experience a breakthrough—we want to know. Your story matters.

Let's move from inspiration to action.

Reach out to us:

📨 To Connect – connect@teamsuccessnetwork.com

📨 Share What God Is Doing – results@teamsuccessnetwork.com

📨 Send Us Documents or Team Reports – docs@teamsuccessnetwork.com

📨 Write Elijah Personally – elijah@teamsuccessnetwork.com

You're not alone in this. The Kingdom is advancing—and we're building it together. Let's keep going.